THIS
BRUTAL
WORLD

THIS
BRUTAL

This Brutal World is my Oyster

My fascination with concrete, industrial landscapes, and what I later came to know as 'Brutalism', started at an early age. It's hardly surprising as I grew up in the North East of England in the late 1970s. At the time, British Steel and the ICI chemical plant commanded the north and eastern flanks of Middlesbrough, the town in which I was born and raised. These chemical and steel plants not only dominated the horizon beyond the town centre, they also supplied an industrial soundtrack of relentless clattering metal. It would be fair to say that the collision of this industrial landscape and of sheet metal audio has shaped and informed my taste both in architecture and music. It has also served me well as a regular source of inspiration in my work as a graphic designer and my unceasing photographic documentation of Brutalist architecture.

William, my grandfather, was a steel worker at the Dorman Long blast furnace in Lackenby, near Redcar [01]. On a bitterly cold day in the winter of 1974, while on one of our regular visits to his place of work, I noticed for the first time — through the rear window of my father's white Ford Anglia — the Dorman Long Coke Oven Tower in South Bank. This industrial monolith, designed by the engineering firm Simon-Carves Limited, was the first concrete building to make a lasting impression on me. Uncompromising and faceless, the structure fuelled my imagination. At such a young age I didn't realise it was possible to build something so tall and so imposing using only concrete. It is testament to the strength and resilience of this building material, despite the structure being over sixty years old, that it still stands proud over the now desolate space that surrounds it.

On any given cold and grey Sunday afternoon in the 1970s my brother Simon and I would be offered a choice: a drive to the North Yorkshire countryside, or to go and see 'the works'. More often than not the latter was our destination of choice. Standing adjacent to British Steel, 'the works', formally known as the ICI chemical plant at Wilton, was a hulking mass of impossibly tangled pipes and cylinders, topped off by ominous plumes of smoke, continually forced skyward via a mass of metallic chimneys [02]. By night, however, it became a different world altogether, transforming itself into a shimmering, industrial flame-lit Las Vegas. This view inspired others, including film director Ridley Scott, also a native of the North East, who based the flaring chimneys in the opening scenes of Blade Runner on the ICI plant in Wilton.

By this time the broader architectural landscape was changing. Just a few years earlier, in 1966, the architecture critic Reyner Banham had used the term 'Brutalism' in his essay *The New Brutalism: Ethic or Aesthetic?* The term gained currency and was used to refer to the style of architecture that was increasingly becoming popular throughout the UK, as well as in France, Germany, Japan, the USA, Canada, Brazil, Israel and Australia. Often commissioned by governmental, cultural and institutional clients, Brutalist architecture was becoming a popular solution for low cost housing, shopping centres, university campus structures and government buildings.

But it wasn't just economic efficiency that concrete construction and Brutalism offered. The architects who favoured it loved the material's 'honesty', the sculptural opportunities, the uncompromising modernity as well as the socially progressive intentions that lay behind the style in a climate of economic decline, political unrest and, in Europe, the long decades of post-war reconstruction.

01

02

These new Brutalist buildings, while addressing very different needs, were as functional, imposing and muscular as the industrial towers of the North East.

I became increasingly fascinated by the visionary buildings and bold housing estates that grew out of the bombed remnants of London's east end. Not always a comfortable fit in their post-war Victorian surroundings, these new concrete buildings and social-housing developments looked, at times, as though they had descended from another planet to colonize Earth. But, while many architects were inspired by the social and aesthetic possibilities of Brutalism, the public's reaction was often hostile. Some Brutalist structures came to be associated with the blight of urban decay as the buildings aged and were badly maintained. The concrete tended to weather poorly, especially in cold northern climates, and as they decayed the buildings became targets for vandalism and graffiti.

What the popular perception overlooked, however, was the utopian ideology that genuinely sought to transform and modernize living and working conditions. Not surprisingly, these social ambitions also resonated in what was then the communist bloc in eastern Europe where Brutalism flourished from the 1960s in Bulgaria, Czechoslovakia, Eastern Germany and Russia. Notable examples include the Ministry of Highways in Georgia (page 119), the Plac Grunwaldzki Apartment Buildings in Poland (page 76) the Design Institute for Robotics and Technical Cybernetics in Russia (page 206) and in the spectacular Druzhba Sanitarium in the Ukraine (page 186).

Regardless of its political origins and social ambitions, the aesthetic power of Brutalist architecture is undeniable. In the 60s and 70s, many architects chose to employ the Brutalist style, even when working with large budgets and private clients purely for the sheer mass and majesty

it offered. In the work of architects such as Marcel Breuer, Le Corbusier, Louis Kahn and Paul Rudolph, Brutalism found its highest expression. Some of the iconic works of the style include Breuer's Saint John's Abbey Church in the USA (page 79), Le Corbusier's Unité d'Habitation in France (page 107), Kahn's National Capital Complex in Bangladesh (page 144) and Rudolph's Faculty of Art and Architecture building at Yale (page 213).

While Brutalist architecture originally took root in Britain, continental Europe and the United States in particular, its seeds were scattered across the globe. Brutalism became popular in Australia, for example the CBC St Leonards Centre, in Sydney (page 81), in Argentina, with outstanding work from Clorindo Testa including the Bank of London and South America in Buenos Aires (page 26), in Brazil where Lina Bo Bardi's São Paulo Museum of Art in São Paulo is the supreme example (page 190) and Japan where Kenzo Tange, among others, took Brutalism to a new level, for example in the Kagawa Prefecture Gymnasium in Kagawa (page 18).

Closer to home, on the handful of times I visited it, the concrete cubist spaceship of the Apollo Pavilion, designed by the British artist Victor Pasmore, transported me to a galaxy far, far away [03]. The pavilion was named after the first manned mission to the moon in 1969, the year the structure was built. You could play in it and climb on it, although it was unforgiving on the knees. Without doubt, its sharp edges, ninety-degree angles and straight lines kick-started my interest and enthusiasm for all things 'Brutal' long before I had heard the word. It was the first building of its kind I had ever seen. From that moment on I fell in love with raw concrete.

Later, aged nine, I remember that on one of my first trips to Newcastle, marvelling at the recently opened futuristic

03

04

Eldon Square Shopping Centre. After yet another 'Are we there yet?' I unwittingly had my first real 'Brutalist' experience. The horizon on the River Tyne, as you enter the city, was once dominated by the Owen Luder Partnership-designed Trinity Square carpark [04]. Blink and you definitely wouldn't have missed this uncompromising hunk of sublime concrete. Both gracious and forthright, this sadly now demolished structure became one of my most cherished Brutalist buildings. I remember my first sight of it looming in the distance and asking my mum 'What's that?' I had never seen anything like it. The structure was thrilling and scary, and I immediately liked it, although I wasn't quite sure why.

Trinity Square carpark was already a star in its own right, after featuring in the 1971 film *Get Carter* starring Michael Caine, a movie I would later go on to watch many times. Remote control in one hand, I was always ready and waiting to pause the VHS at the various points in the film whenever this concrete beast loomed.

Owen Luder, the architect of a number of controversial Brutalist buildings in the UK, was also responsible for another landmark on the Gateshead skyline: the twenty-nine-storey Derwent Tower, also known as the Dunston Rocket [05]. Luder's designs were some of the most powerful and raw examples of Brutalist architecture, characterized by massive sculptural concrete forms devoid of claddings or decoration. The cold, damp British climate, combined with poor maintenance, however, exacerbated the unpopularity of his buildings, despite a number of them winning prestigious architecture awards when they were built. Derwent Tower, along with Trinity Square's older sibling, the Tricorn in Portsmouth [06], also by Luder, have all suffered the same fate. These once heroic, visionary buildings were all demolished between 2004 and 2012.

In recent years, Owen Luder's work, along with Brutalist architecture in general, has seen a mass resurgence in popularity among those who see in these buildings not the failed dreams of an older generation of architects but a vision of a society that was confident in its own expression, a society that gave us an architecture of a generous, open and radical welfare state. Perhaps the new-found public interest in the once derided Brutalist style and the race to preserve these buildings, had it emerged just a few years earlier, could have saved Owen Luder's Brutalist trio from demolition. My Trinity Square thankfully lives on in 1971 Technicolor glory.

By the time I was sixteen, my interest in electronic music was gathering pace. I had my first introduction to the music of Joy Division and the accompanying artwork designed by Peter Saville. The repetitive imagery and ordered components on the LP sleeve of *Unknown Pleasures* left a lasting impression on me, and became a source of inspiration for my burgeoning interest in graphic design and photography.

During my studies at Cleveland College of Art and Design, I was introduced to the work of the Bauhaus architect, Marcel Breuer. I particularly liked the strong shapes and patterns he set in concrete on the surfaces of the buildings he designed. Just as wonderful were the bold geometric shape-shifting angular shadows cast by these buildings on the land that surrounded them. I saw direct parallels between these concrete surface patterns and the record sleeves I loved, as well as in the grid systems created by Josef Müller-Brockmann and Wim Crouwel, graphic designers who I had recently been introduced to at art college. My discovery of Marcel Breuer sparked memories of a school skiing trip a few years earlier.

Turning off the autoroute near Chamonix, the 1970s deluxe coach — my home for the last thirty hours — made its

05

06

its way cautiously along the snowy mountain roads of the Haute Savoie region in south east France. Flaine, which nestles against the borders of Switzerland and Italy, was our destination. But the faux Tyrolean pitched roof buildings I had expected were nowhere to be seen. Instead, I was greeted by an imposing cluster of modern buildings glinting in the late morning sunshine. I felt immediately at ease in my temporary surroundings, and the language of these buildings felt strangely familiar to me, as someone who had clambered over the Apollo Pavilion as a kid.

Flaine was the brainchild of Eric Boissonas, a geophysical engineer, his modern art-loving wife Sylvie and a supporting cast who included architect-in-chief Marcel Breuer. Conceived in 1959 and opened a decade later, Flaine also boasts a number of sculptures: *La Téte de Femme* by Pablo Picasso, *Le Boqueteau* by Jean Dubuffet and *Les Trois Hexagones* by Victor Vasarely — the latter stood outside the hotel I was staying in.

The jewel in Flaine's concrete crown is the cantilevered Hotel La Flaine, which clings precariously to a craggy rock wall [07]. Therein lies the genius of Marcel Breuer and the beauty of Flaine — the ease with which these concrete monoliths fit seamlessly into the most natural of surroundings. The winter sport was a great experience. However, it was the buildings that made a more profound impression on me, long after the euphoria of learning to ski had subsided. It was only later, sitting in the library at art college, that I realised with delight that I had stayed in a Marcel Breuer-designed hotel.

My second 'Brutalist' experience occurred when I was a teenager, a good few years after the childhood epiphany of my first exposure to the style via Trinity Square Car Park in Gateshead. I was on the way to Sheffield for a night of unadulterated electronic hedonism, and from the comfort of my plush upholstered coach seat I enjoyed a bird's eye view of the city. Set against a grey Yorkshire sky, the imposing complex of radical concrete buildings known as the Park Hill and Hyde Park Estates which were set on one of the city's seven hills, dominated the horizon. The sheer scale of these social housing estates was overwhelming and breathtaking. Park Hill [08] opened in 1961 and was designed by Jack Lynn and Ivor Smith, who were inspired by Le Corbusier's Unité d'Habitation in Marseilles (page 107) and the work of British architects Alison and Peter Smithson who were closely associated with the New Brutalism movement. Park Hill was Grade II listed in 1998, saving it from the fate that befell Hyde Park which was demolished in 1991. Beyond the current regeneration of Park Hill, its dystopian former self was immortalized by Jarvis Cocker and Pulp in their 1992 track 'Sheffield: Sex City'.

After the break up of The Jam in 1982, I had found myself on the look out for something else to sonically entertain me. By now I was worshipping at a different musical altar altogether, an electronic one that originated in the city of Sheffield where Pulp started out. The Human League and Heaven 17 were undoubtedly great, however the band I really fell in love with was Cabaret Voltaire. From the Neville Brody-designed record sleeves for their *Micro-Phonies* album, through to the appearance of the Tinsley Viaduct towers [09] in their 'Sensoria' video, this was music for the future, with repetitive beats inspired by the sounds emanating from the local drop forges. It was a sound that was a product of its time and its surroundings, and I was captivated. This love affair has endured, in part due to releases in the mid-nineties by Warp Records, including genre-defining releases by LFO, Nightmares on Wax, Autechre and Aphex Twin.

07

08

09

As these artists replaced those of my youth, so new architects created new buildings that supplemented, in my affections, those I had grown up with. No longer described using the term Brutal, none the less, architects such as Zaha Hadid, Peter Zumthor, Daniel Libeskind and Tadao Ando were making their presence felt in the 1990s in a new kind of architecture freed from any '-isms'. Instead a variety of loose terminologies — 'neo-futurist', 'minimalist', 'critical regionalist' and even 'deconstructivist' — were being employed instead. While broadly individualist in approach, it can be argued that some of the work of this new breed of contemporary architects had its origins in that of the original Brutalists, not least in their often monumental form-making and in their austere use of singular materials and forms, especially concrete. This can be seen, for example, in Zumthor's Brother Claus Chapel in Germany (page 42) and Ando's Roberto Garza Sada Center for Arts in Mexico (page 22), both sublime works in concrete that clearly exhibit traces of the Brutalist style.

Concrete and music have become enduring features in my life over the past twenty-five years. My early days in London were spent attempting to skate the harsh angled banks underneath the Hayward Gallery [10] and Queen Elizabeth Hall. Situated on the South Bank of the Thames the Southbank skatepark was, and remains, one of the most hallowed skating destinations in London. It used to be a hostile place to visit in those days, certainly not the brightly painted user-friendly 'Brutalist' arts centre it is today.

My newly acquired job of designing record sleeves (still my profession today), quickly became an outlet for my re-discovered interest in photography. I started to document my travels around London and further afield. Firstly pointing the lens at anything of interest to me, then increasingly at buildings, concrete, and particularly the defined straight edges and dominant structures from the Brutalist movement. The Barbican Estate in the City of London became an early muse. To this day I make regular visits with my camera and always manage to seek out yet another new viewpoint. When it opened in 1982, Queen Elizabeth declared it to be 'one of the modern wonders of the world', and I am more than inclined to agree. The ambition and vision within the Barbican site is awe-inspiring. It continues to amaze me how the architects, Chamberlin, Powell and Bon, managed to intricately knit together a utopian vision for this formerly scarred bomb-site in the city.

Before I moved to London in 1988 to study at the Chelsea School of Art, I had only seen Trellick Tower in a late 70s episode of The Professionals. The Professionals was a Sunday night favourite of mine. This particular episode is a Modernist time capsule containing footage not only of Trellick Tower but also of the Westway, along with a supporting cast of housing estates and tower blocks from all corners of London. Designed by Ernö Goldfinger and opened in 1972, Trellick Tower near Ladbroke Grove in west London became a constant backdrop to the early years in my newly adopted city [11]. I lived and worked near the thirty-one-storey tower for a number of years throughout the 1990s. The tower's imposing silhouette was ever-present at this time along with my Sony Discman and a bag full of Acid House CDs.

After ten years of living in west London I found myself thrust into the pre-gentrified eastern side of the city. I immediately liked it and felt at home. Moving east, appropriately in the year 2000, I discovered my spiritual home, along with some fine examples of post-war architecture. In my new surroundings, armed with my camera and an insatiable appetite for all things concrete, modern, post-war and 'Brutal'. I began to photograph

10   11

a wealth of wonderfully bold and confident buildings. They all had heroic-sounding names that rolled off your tongue, such as Lasdun, Lubetkin and the previously mentioned Goldfinger. I felt spoilt. Buildings by this cast of architectural greats could be found just a short walk or bus ride from my new home. The band Saint Etienne eloquently captured the spirit of these architects in the lyrics of their track 'When I was Seventeen': 'Lubetkin, Corbusier, van Der Rohe, Mendelssohn. Modern, modern, Brutalist architecture. Future, future, the future is clean and modern.'

Having amassed an extensive archive of photographs over the years that now runs into the tens of thousands, I set about sorting this growing collection of digital images into sections entitled: 'Brutalism', 'Modernism', 'Concrete' and 'Post-War'. This is still a work in progress. In 2014 I decided to set up a Twitter account so that I could share images from my archive, specifically the Brutalist ones, along with music and anything else that caught my eye. A broad canvas, but one that is representative of my work, bringing together all the stuff that inspires me, and just as importantly, the things that I like. Next, the name. It was an easy decision with only one contender. One of the first house records I bought was released on the Cooltempo label in 1987. The track, 'This Brutal House' by Nitro Deluxe was an early favourite of mine from the beginning of the acid house revolution. I always loved the track name and thought that one day I would appropriate it.

Decisions made, the @BrutalHouse Twitter feed was born and my first tweet was sent in March from the newly created account. I wasn't sure what to expect but any early doubts were quickly dispelled, with the feed attracting 1,000 enthusiastic followers within a little under two months. It seemed there were other like-minded people out there, with a love of Brutalist architecture.

Which is why I decided to create this book. It is both an homage to Brutalism and a visual manifesto that celebrates this awe-inspiring style of architecture. I wanted to take the opportunity to reinvent and reappraise the term 'Brutal'. To celebrate the very best of the traditional canon of Brutalism, bring to light many virtually unknown Brutalist architectural treasures that I have come across in my real and virtual travels over the years and also to propose that Brutalism lives on in so much contemporary architecture of the late twentieth and early twenty-first centuries.

As I have come to realize, Brutalism is a truly global architectural phenomenon. In the following pages we travel to Argentina, Australia and Azerbaijan — Canada, Chile and China — Georgia, Germany and Guatemala — Iceland, India and Israel — Nepal, North Korea and Norway — Paraguay, Peru and Poland — Serbia, Singapore and Sweden — as well as locations right across eastern and western Europe and the United States. These pages are also a testament to the fact that, perhaps finally, Brutalism can now shed its sense of danger and has come full circle, from utopia, to dystopia and back again. Whereas once so much of the world's Brutalist architectural heritage was neglected, unloved and in danger of being torn down and relegated to land fill, now, here in this book, we can celebrate the power and beauty of this most compelling style of architecture. This Brutal world is my oyster.

Peter Chadwick

'THE MINISTRY OF TRUTH ... WAS AN ENORMOUS PYRAMIDAL STRUCTURE OF GLITTERING WHITE CONCRETE, SOARING UP TERRACE AFTER TERRACE, THREE HUNDRED METRES INTO THE AIR. A THOUSAND ROCKET BOMBS WOULD NOT BATTER IT DOWN.'

—

GEORGE ORWELL

← Hemeroscopium House, Madrid, Spain, 2008
by Ensamble Studio (previous pages).

↑ Reading Space, Jinhua Architecture Park, Jinhua,
China, 2006 by Herzog & de Meuron.

→ Temple Street Parking Garage, New Haven,
Connecticut, USA, 1961 by Paul Rudolph.

'Popular opinion swayed
against Brutalism far before the neo-
liberalists, when the anti-Establishment
generation of the 60s accused
Rudolph's buildings of being "Fascist".'

— Timothy Rohan

'There is a powerful need
for symbolism, and that means the
architecture must have something
that appeals to the human heart.'

— Kenzo Tange

↑ Kagawa Prefecture Gymnasium, Kagawa,
   Japan, 1964 by Kenzo Tange Associates.

→ Memorial and Cultural Centre, Kolašin,
   Montenegro, 1975 by Marko Mušič.

'The drive for monumentality is as inbred as the desire for food and sex, regardless of how we denigrate it. Monuments differ in different periods. Each age has its own.'

— Philip Johnson

↖ Bank of Guatemala, Guatemala City, Guatemala, 1966 by Jorge Montes Córdova and Raúl Minondo.

↑ Ministerio de Educación, Lima, Peru, 2012 by DLPS.

→ Jenaro Valverde Marín Building, CCSS, San José, Costa Rica, 1976 by Alberto Linner Díaz.

→ Concrete House, Buenos Aires, Argentina, 2007, BAK Arquitectos.
↓ Roberto Garza Sada Center for Arts, Architecture and Design (CRGS), Monterrey University UDEM, Monterrey, Mexico, 2012 by Tadao Ando.

→ Vodafone Headquarters Building Oporto, Porto, Portugal, 2006 by Barbosa & Guimarães Arquitectos.

CENTRO ROBER

'I don't think that architecture is only
about shelter, is only about a very simple
enclosure. It should be able to excite you,
to calm you, to make you think.'

— Zaha Hadid

'Brutalism's opponents dare
not simply own up to disliking
the look of the stuff.'

— Jonathan Meades

↖ Hawaii State Capitol, Honolulu, Hawaii,
   USA, 1969 by John Carl Warnecke & Associates
   and Belt, Lemmon & Lo.
← Faculty of Law, UDG (Universitat de Girona),
   Girona, Spain, 2006 by RCR Arquitectes and
   BG Arquitectes.

↑ Transformer Station, Budapest, Hungary, 1969
   by Ernö Léstyán.
→ Museum aan de Stroom, Antwerp, Belgium, 2010
   by Neutelings Riedijk Architects.

← Bank of London and South America, Buenos Aires, Argentina, 1966 by Clorindo Testa & SEPRA.

→ Belgacom Building (RTT Tower), Ghent, Belgium, 1971 by George and Dirk Bontinck.

↘ Nakagin Capsule Tower, Tokyo, Japan, 1972 by Kisho & Kurokawa Architect & Associates.

27

↑ Thermal Power Station and Central Control Cabin,
   Florence, Italy, 1934 by Angiolo Mazzoni.
↗ Bergisel Ski Jump, Innsbruck, Austria, 2002
   by Zaha Hadid Architects.

→ St. Joseph's Hospital, Tacoma, Washington,
   USA, 1974, Bertrand Goldberg.

'Thirty thousand feet above the earth / It's a beautiful thing / Everybody's a beautiful thing / Mmm skyscraper I love you'

— Underworld, 'Mmm Skyscraper I Love You'

← Hong Kong Club, Hong Kong, China, 1984 by Harry Seidler & Associates.

↑ Kanchanjunga Apartments, Mumbai, India, 1983 by Charles Correa Associates.

↗ Overseas Chinese Banking Corporation Centre, Singapore, Singapore, 1976 by I. M. Pei and Partners.

← Ryugyong Hotel, Pyongyang, North Korea, 2012,
Baikdoosan Architects & Engineers.

↑ Cadet Chapel, United States Air Force Academy,
Colorado Springs, Colorado, USA, 1963
by Skidmore, Owings & Merrill (SOM).

↖ Power Plant, Røldal, Norway, 1965 by Geir Grung.
↖ Via Azul House, Santiago, Chile, 2005 by
Guillermo Acuña Arquitectos Asociados.
← 'The Egg', Center for the Performing Arts, Albany,
New York, USA, 1978 by Wallace Harrison.

↑ Sydney Masonic Centre (SMC), Sydney, New
South Wales, Australia, 1979 by Joseland Gilling.
→ Prentice Women's Hospital, Chicago, Illinois,
USA, 1975 by Bertrand Goldberg.

'Contact with Brutalist architecture tends to drive one to hard judgements.'

— Reyner Banham

↑   Notre Dame de Royan, Royan, France, 1958 by Guillaume Gillet.
←   Radio Kootwijk, Kootwijk, The Netherlands, 1923 by Julius Maria Luthmann.

→   Edificio Asuguradora del Valle, Bogotá, Colombia, 1972 by ARK.

'IN ORDER TO BE
BRUTALIST, A BUILDING
HAS TO MEET THREE CRITERIA,
NAMELY THE CLEAR EXHIBITION
OF STRUCTURE, THE
VALUATION OF MATERIALS
"AS FOUND" AND
MEMORABILITY AS IMAGE.'

—

REYNER BANHAM

'Forget your perfect offering /
There is a crack in everything /
That's how the light gets in'

— Leonard Cohen

→ Zalman Aranne Central Library, Ben-Gurion
University of the Negev, Beer-Sheva, Israel, 1975
by Shmuel Bixon, Moshe Gil and Shimshon Amitai.

42

← Brother Claus Chapel, Mechernich, Germany,
2007 by Peter Zumthor.

↑ Igualada Cemetery Park, Barcelona, Spain,
1991 by Carme Pinós and Enric Miralles.

'The organization of light and shadow effects
produce a new enrichment of vision.'

— László Moholy-Nagy

← Beinecke Rare Book and Manuscript Library,
New Haven, Connecticut, USA, 1963 by Gordon
Bunshaft and Skidmore, Owings, & Merrill (SOM).

↑ Concert Hall, León, Spain, 2002 by Mansilla
& Tuñón Arquitectos.
→ City Hall, Chemnitz, Germany, 1974 by Rudolf
Weißer.

'It seemed like a nice neighborhood
to have bad habits in.'

— Raymond Chandler

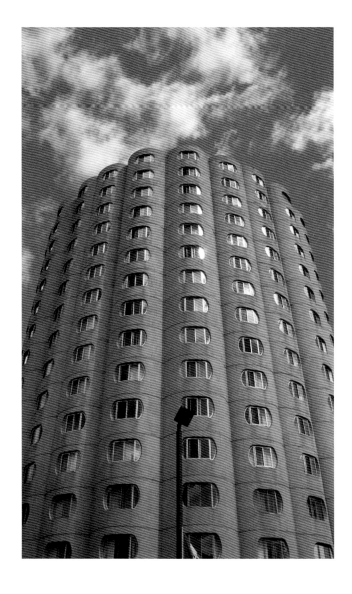

↖ HUD Building, Washington DC, USA, 1968
by Marcel Breuer.
← Learning Hub, Nanyang Technological University,
Singapore, 2015 by Heatherwick Studio.

↑ Raymond Hilliard Homes, Chicago, Illinois,
USA, 1966 by Bertrand Goldberg.
↗ Aillaud Towers (Tours Nuage), Nanterre,
France, 1977 by Emile Aillaud.

'Lubetkin, Corbusier, van der Rohe, Mendelssohn /
Modern, modern, brutalist architecture /
Future, future, the future is clean and modern'

— Saint Etienne, 'When I Was Seventeen'

↑   Chapel of Notre-Dame-du-Haut, Ronchamp,
    France, 1955 by Le Corbusier.

→   Casar de Cáceres Bus Station, Cáceres, Spain,
    2003 by Justo Garciá Rubio.

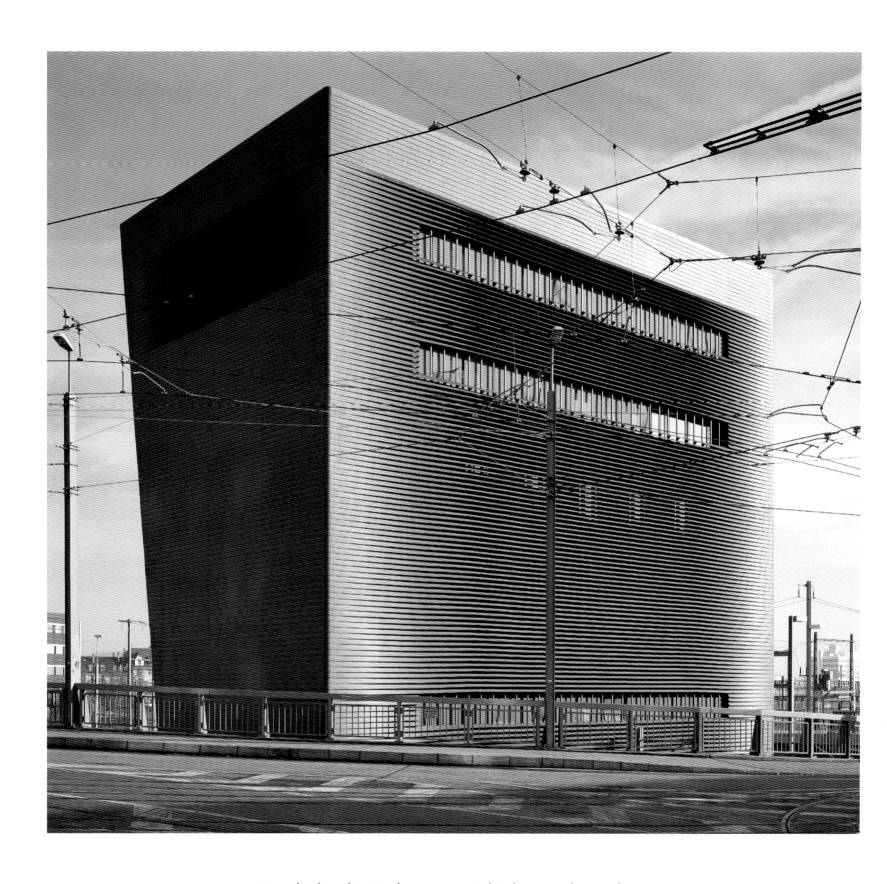

'Frank Lloyd Wright once said "doctors bury their
mistakes but architects can only grow vines over them".
Banksy once added "that was before they invented
500 ml cans of extra wide chrome paint".'

– Banksy

↖ Signal Box, Basel, Switzerland, 1994 by
Herzog & de Meuron.

→ SC Johnson Wax Research Tower, Racine,
Wisconsin, USA, 1939 by Frank Lloyd Wright.

← Hochbunker Pallasstraße, Berlin, Germany, 1945 and Pallasseum Housing, 1977 by Jürgen Sawade.

→ Bilbao Exhibition Centre (BEC), Bilbao, Spain, 2007 by ACXT.

↓ Embassy of Russia, Havana, Cuba 1985 by Aleksandr Rochegov.

↘ Misfits Tower, Anyang Art Park, Anyang, South Korea, 2005 by Didier Fiuza Faustino, Bureau des Mésarchitectures.

← House in San Abbondio, San Abbondio,
Switzerland, 2012 by Wespi de Meuron Romeo
Architekten.
↓ Eglise Saint-Nicolas, Hérémence, Switzerland, 1971
by Walter Maria Förderer.

→ Erie Basin Marina Observation Tower, Buffalo,
New York, USA, 1973 by DiDonato Associates.

'I think all good architecture
should challenge you, make you
start asking questions.
You don't have to understand it.
You may not like it. That's OK.'

— Thom Mayne

← Clifton Cathedral, Bristol, England, UK, 1973
by Percy Thomas Partnership.
↓ Basilica of Our Lady of Coromoto, Guanare,
Venezuela, 1996 by Erasmo Calvani.

→ Trellick Tower, London, England, UK, 1972
by Ernö Goldfinger.
↘ Genex Tower, Belgrade, Serbia, 1977 by
Mihajlo Mitrović.

'Later, as he sat on his balcony eating the dog, Dr Robert Laing reflected on the unusual events that had taken place within this huge apartment building during the previous three months.'

— J G Ballard, *High Rise*

↑ Town Hall, Bremen, Germany, 1964 by Roland
Rainer with Säume & Hafermann.
→ Dollan Aqua Centre, East Kilbride, Scotland,
UK, 1968 by Alexander Buchanan Campbell.

↗ Indoor Tennis Stadium, Tashkent,
Uzbekistan, 1997 by Valeri Akopjanian.
→ State Industrial and Technical Institute (ITIS),
Busto Arsizio, Italy, 1965 by Enrico Castiglioni
and Carlo Fontana.

← Praxis, Mexico City, Mexico, 1975 by Agustín Hernández.

→ Rehabilitation Centre, Dombai, Russia, 1985.
↓ Army Pavillion, Expo64, Lausanne, Switzerland, 1964 by Jan Roth.

← Bio-Towers, Lauchhammer, Germany, 1957.
Renovations in 2008 by Jähne & Göpfert
and Zimmermann & Partner.
↙ Ark Building, Kyoto, Japan, 1983 by Shin
Takamatsu Architect and Associates.

→ Auditorium Maurice Ravel, Lyon, France, 1975
by Henry Pottier and Charles Delfante.
↓ Dingleton Boiler House, Melrose, Scotland,
UK, 1977 by Peter Womersley.

'Architecture should speak
of its time and place,
but yearn for timelessness.'

— Frank Gehry

'ALL THE MAJESTY OF
A CITY LANDSCAPE /
ALL THE SOARING DAYS OF
OUR LIVES / ALL THE
CONCRETE DREAMS
IN MY MINDS EYE / ALL THE
JOY I SEE THROUGH
THESE ARCHITECT'S EYES'

—

DAVID BOWIE

↑ National Monument to the Resistance, Plateau des Glières, France, 1973 by Émile Giliolo.

→ Municipal Office Leyweg, The Hague, The Netherlands, 2011 by Rudy Uytenhaak Architectenbureau.

'The Brutalist citizen has to be understood as an abstract egalitarian ideal, not as an individual lost in a microscopic concrete cave of some gargantuan building.'

— Jack Self

← Park Hill, Sheffield, England, UK, 1961 by Ivor Smith and Jack Lynn.

↗ Satellite Towers, Mexico City, Mexico, 1957 by Luis Barragán and Mathias Goeritz.

'The whole city getting stiff in the
building heat / ... Everyone on Park Hill
came in unison at four-thirteen a.m.'

— Pulp, 'Sheffield: Sex City'

↑ National Gymnasium for Tokyo Olympics, Tokyo, Japan, 1964 by Kenzo Tange Associates.
← Indoor Sports Arena of Saint-Nazaire (La Soucoupe), Saint-Nazaire, France, 1970 by Vissuzaine, Longuet, Rivière et Joly.

↗ Falkirk Wheel & Visitor Centre, Edinburgh, Scotland, UK, 2002 by RMJM.
↗ Long Museum (West Bund), Shanghai, China, 2014 by Atelier Deshaus.
→ Cross of the Third Millenium, Coquimbo, Chile, 2000 by Carlos Aguirre Mandiola, Carlos Aguirre Baeza, Juan Pablo Parentini Gayani and Álvaro Páez Rivera.

'The question isn't
who is going to let me;
it's who is going to stop me.'

— Ayn Rand

72

'Architecture can't fully represent the chaos and turmoil that are part of the human personality, but you need to put some of that turmoil into the architecture, or it isn't real.'

— Frank Stella

← Boston City Hall, Boston, Massachusetts, USA, 1969 by Kallmann, McKinnell & Knowles and Campbell, Aldrich & Nulty (previous pages).

→ RMIT Design Hub, Melbourne, Victoria, Australia, 2012 by Sean Godsell Architects.
↓ M House, Gorman, California, USA, 2000 by Michael Jantzen.

→ Jewish Museum Berlin, Berlin, Germany, 2001 by Daniel Libeskind.

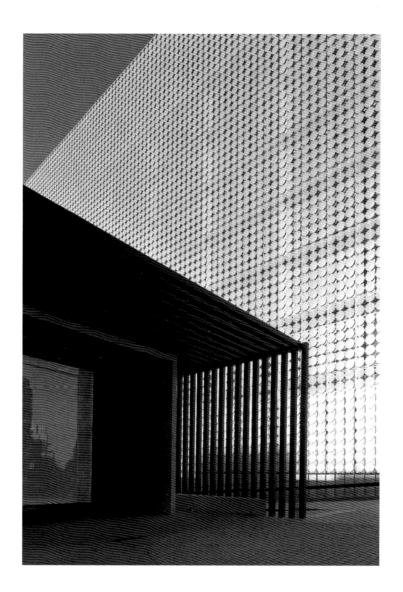

↖ Plac Grunwaldzki Apartment Buildings, Wrocław,
Poland, 1975 by Jadwiga Grabowska-Hawrylak.
↑ The Three Towers of Grenoble, Grenoble,
France, 1967 by Roger Anger and Pierre Puccinelli.
← Convalescent Home, Tiberias, Israel, 1973
by Arieh Sharon and Eldar Sharon.

↗ Coal Silo, Madrid, Spain, 1951 by Eduardo Torroja,
Manuel Barbero and Gonzalo Echegaray.
↗ Synagogue in the Negev Desert, Military Academy,
Negev Desert, Israel, 1969 by Zvi Hecker
and Alfred Neumann.
→ Ramot Housing, Jerusalem, Israel, 1975 by
Zvi Hecker.

'A new language requires a new technique. If what you're saying doesn't require a new language, then what you're saying probably isn't new.'

— Philip Glass

↖ Negev Monument, Beersheva, Israel, 1968
by Dani Karavan.
← La Plage du Pacifique Hotel, Vanuatu Resort,
Vanuatu, 2013 by Kristin Green.

↑ Saint John's Abbey Church, Collegeville,
Minnesota, USA, 1961 by Marcel Breuer.

← The Mirador House, Casablanca, Chile, 2015 by
   Víctor Gubbins Browne & Gubbins Arquitectos.
↙ Habitat '67 Apartment Building, Montréal, Québec,
   Canada, 1967 by Moshe Safdie.

→ Heat Plant, Uithof University Campus, Utrecht,
   The Netherlands, 2005 by Zeinstra van der Pol,
   DOK Architecten.
↓ CBC St Leonards Centre, Sydney, New South
   Wales, Australia, 1972 by Kerr & Smith Architects.

← Louis Nucéra Library, Nice, France, 2002 by
  Bayard et Chapus (architects) and Sosno (sculptor).

→ State Trading Corporation (STC), New Delhi,
  India, 1989 by Raj Rewal.
↓ J Edgar Hoover FBI Building, Washington DC,
  USA, 1974 by Charles F Murphy and Associates.

'No future they say /
But must it be that way /
Now is calling /
The city is human'

— The Human League,
'Blind Youth'

↑ Armstrong Rubber Company Building (The Pirelli
Tire Building), New Haven, Connecticut,
USA, 1968 by Marcel Breuer and Robert F Gatje.

→ Tiwag Power Station Control Centre, Silz, Austria,
2014 by Bechter Zaffignani Architekten.

'They swore by concrete.
They built for eternity.'

— Günter Grass, *The Tin Drum*

'A building has integrity, just as a man and just as seldom. It must be true to its own idea, have its own form, and serve its own purpose.'

— Ayn Rand

← Shrine of the Virgin of 'La Antigua', Alberite,
   La Rioja, Spain, 2009 by Otxotorena Arquitectos.
↙ Casa del Fascio, Como, Italy, 1936 by Giuseppe
   Terragni.

→ House 20, Melbourne, Victoria, Australia, 2010
   by Jolson Architecture.
↓ Town Hall, Marl, Germany, 1967 by Van den
   Broek and Bakema.

← Dutch Reformed Church, Rijsenhout, The Netherlands, 2006 by Claus en Kaan Architecten.
↓ Sancaklar Mosque, Istanbul, Turkey, 2012 by Emre Arolat Architects.

→ Siddhartha Children & Women Hospital, Butwal, Nepal, 1998 by Tadao Ando.

'No architecture can be truly noble
which is not imperfect.'

— John Ruskin

'DO IT FOR THE PIECE
OF SKY WE ARE STEALING
WITH OUR BUILDING.
YOU DO IT FOR THE AIR
THAT WILL BE DISPLACED,
AND MOST OF ALL,
YOU DO IT FOR THE FUCKING
CONCRETE. BECAUSE
IT IS DELICATE AS BLOOD.'

—

IVAN LOCKE

↑ Waterside Plaza, New York, New York,
USA, 1974 by Davis, Brody & Associates.

→ Kaiser Wilhelm Memorial Church, Berlin,
Germany, 1963 by Egon Eiermann.

'A hundred times have I thought
New York is a catastrophe and fifty times:
It is a beautiful catastrophe.'

— Le Corbusier

'Brutalism is back, we have learned
to love concrete chic.'

— Oliver Wainwright

← Extension Añorbe Cemetery, Añorbe, Spain,
  2011 by MRM Arquitectos.
↙ Living Madrid, Madrid, Spain, 2008
  by Wiel Arets Architects.

→ Sanchinarro Mirador Apartments, Madrid,
  Spain, 2005 by MVRDV.
↓ Pandion Vista, Cologne, Germany, 2011
  by Hadi Teherani BRT Architekten.

'Brutalism is not so much ruined
as dormant, derelict — still
functioning even in a drastically badly
treated fashion, and as such ready
to be recharged and reactivated.
This rough beast might
still slouch towards a concrete
New Jerusalem.'

— Owen Hatherley

→ Centro de Exposições do Centro Administrativo da
Bahia, Bahia, Brazil, 1974 by João Filgueiras Lima,
(Lelé).

← Timmelsjoch Experience Pass Museum, Timmelsjoch, Austria, 2010 by Werner Tscholl Architekt.
↙ Sunset Chapel, Acapulco, Mexico, 2011 by Bunker Arquitectura.

→ Hotel Le Flaine, Flaine, France, 1968 by Marcel Breuer.
↓ Parish Church of Santa Monica, Madrid, Spain, 2008 by Vicens + Ramos Arquitectos.

'Beauty will be convulsive or it will not be at all.'

— André Breton

↑ SGAE Central Office, Santiago de Compostela, Spain, 2008 by Ensamble Studio.

→ Brion Cemetery, San Vito d'Altivole, Italy, 1977 by Carlo Scarpa.

'A police car and a screamin' siren /
Pneumatic drill and ripped-up concrete'

— The Jam, 'That's Entertainment'

102

← Auditorium, Delft University of Technology, Delft, Netherlands, 1966 by Van den Broek and Bakema.
↙ Wind Barrier, Caland Canal, Rozenburg, The Netherlands, 1985 by Maarten Struijs and Frans de Wit.

→ Americas Mart Building 3, Atlanta, Georgia, USA, 1957 by John Portman & Associates.
↓ Basilica Santuario Madonna delle Lacrime, Syracuse, Sicily, Italy, 1994 by Michel Andrault and Pierre Parat.

'What characterizes the
New Brutalism in architecture ...
is precisely its brutality,
its *je-m'en-foutisme*,
its bloody-mindedness.'

— Reyner Banham

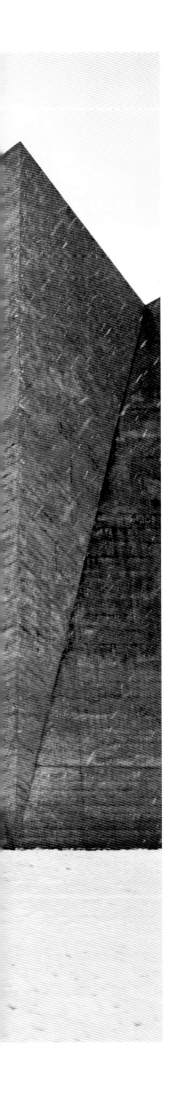

← Basel College of Art and Design
  (former Trade School), Basel, Switzerland,
  1961 by Hermann Baur, Hans Peter Baur,
  Franz Bräuning and Arthur Dürig.

↑ Shirokane House, Tokyo, Japan, 2013
  by MDS.

↑ Solomon R. Guggenheim Museum, New York,
   New York, USA, 1959 by Frank Lloyd Wright.

→ Unité d'Habitation (La Cité Radieuse), Marseille,
   France, 1952 by Le Corbusier.

← Catedral Metropolitana de São Sebastião, Rio de Janeiro, Brazil, 1979 by Edgar Fonseca.
↓ Tsitsernakaberd Memorial Complex, Yerevan, Armenia, 1967 by Arthur Tarkhanyan and Sashur Kalashyan.

→ Grand Central Water Tower, Midrand, South Africa, 1996 by GAPP Architects & Urban Designers.

↑ Church of Santa Maria Immacolata, Longarone, Italy, 1982 by Giovanni Michelucci.
← Church of Seed, Huizhou, China, 2011 by O Studio Architects.

↗ Church of Sainte-Bernadette-du-Banlay, Nevers, France, 1966 by Claude Parent and Paul Virilio.
↗ Trudelturm, Aerodynamic Park, Berlin, Germany, 1936 by Hermann Brenner and Werner Deutschmann.
→ White U, Tokyo, Japan, 1976 by Toyo Ito & Associates.

↑ SILOS 13 – Cement Distribution Centre, Paris,
France, 2014 by VIB Architecture.
→ Cattedrale di Cristo Re, La Spezia, Italy, 1975
by Adalberto Libera and Cesare Galeazzi.

→ Meditation Space, UNESCO, Paris, France,
1995 by Tadao Ando.

'The architecture that we remember is that which never consoles or comforts us.'

— Peter Eisenman

← Mondial House, London, England, UK, 1975
by Hubbard Ford & Partners.
↙ Palmas 555, Mexico City, Mexico, 1975 by
Sordo Madaleno Arquitectos.

→ New Court, Christ's College, Cambridge, England,
UK, 1970 by Denys Lasdun.
↓ Memorial to the Murdered Jews of Europe, Berlin,
Germany, 2005 by Eisenmann Architects.

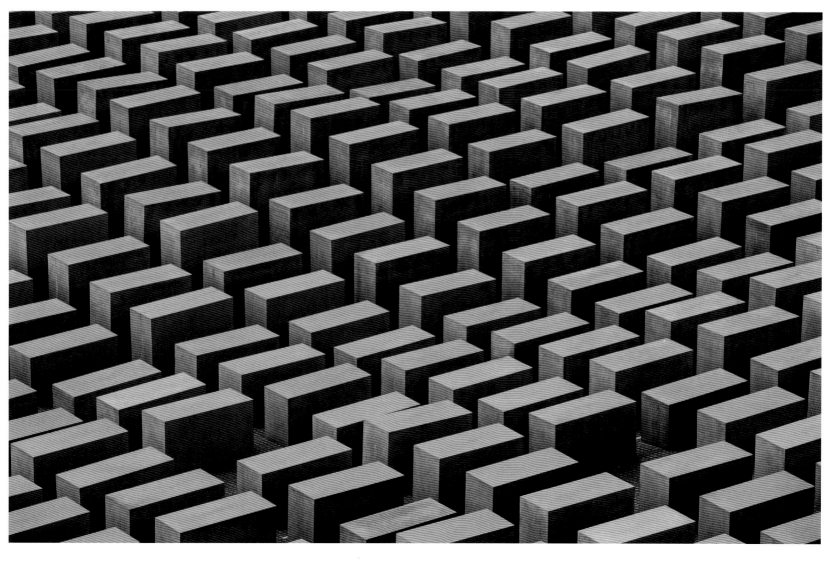

'BRUTALISM TRIES TO FACE
UP TO A MASS-PRODUCTION
SOCIETY, AND DRAG A
ROUGH POETRY OUT OF THE
CONFUSED AND POWERFUL
FORCES WHICH ARE AT WORK.
UP TO NOW BRUTALISM
HAS BEEN DISCUSSED
STYLISTICALLY, WHEREAS
ITS ESSENCE IS ETHICAL.'

—

ALISON AND PETER SMITHSON

'Green, green, the neon green /
New world towers /
Carved out of grey white skies'

— Blur, 'New World Towers'

← The Interlace, Singapore, Singapore, 2013
  by OMA / Ole Scheeren.

→ The Ministry of Highways, Tbilisi, Georgia,
  1974 by Georgy Chakhava.

119

↑ Assembly Building, Chandigarh, India, 1962
by Le Corbusier.

↗ Hirschgarten Skatepark, Munich, Germany, 2010
by BOWL Construction.
→ Selvika National Tourist Route, Finnmark,
Norway, 2012 by Reiulf Ramstad Arkitekter.

'[Brutal architecture] is honest. It is functional, and it reflects what it does. That's why we liked it.'

— Hilla Becher

↑ Roihuvuori Water Tower, Helsinki, Finland, 1977 by Consulting Office Arto Pitkanen.

↗ MLC Centre, Sydney, New South Wales, Australia, 1978 by Harry Seidler and Associates.

→ Monument Ilinden (Makedonium), Krushevo, Macedonia, 1974 by Jordan and Iskra Grabuloski.

↑ Parking Garage, Macy's Queens, Queens, New York, New York, USA, 1965 by Skidmore, Owings & Merrill.

→ Preston Central Bus Station and Car Park, Preston, England, UK, 1969 by Keith Ingham and Charles Wilson.

'A cavernous garage, harshly spot-lit, decorated in self-conscious brutalist chic.'

— *American Psycho*

'Harrow the house of the dead;
look shining at New styles of architecture,
a change of heart.'

— W H Auden

← San Cataldo Cemetery, Modena, Italy, 1984
  by Aldo Rossi.

→ Poli House, Coliumo, Chile, 2005 by Pezo
  von Ellrichshausen.
↓ Musical Studies Centre, Santiago de Compostela,
  Spain, 2002 by Ensamble Studio.

→ Crystal Hall, Baku, Azerbaijan, 2012
by GMP Architekten.

'Two hearts under a skyscraper /
Let's stay together /
Let's stay in this broken down
love / Let's stay together /
Two hearts under the skyscrapers'

— Suede, 'Stay Together'

← New Museum of Contemporary Art, New York, New York, USA, 2007 by SANAA.

→ De Rotterdam, Rotterdam, The Netherlands, 2013 by OMA.

← Canongate Flats, Edinburgh, Scotland, UK, 1969
  by Basil Spence & Partners.

↙ St Bride's Church, East Kilbride, Scotland, UK, 1963
  by Gillespie, Kidd & Coia.

↓ Tricorn Centre, Portsmouth, England, UK, 1966
  by Owen Luder Partnership.

'I find lumps of concrete
like this, sexy.'

— David Adjaye

'Brutalism: challenging, idealistic and serious — Brutalism is architecture for grown ups.'

— Jonathan Meades

← Rainier Square Bank Tower, Seattle, Washington, USA, 1977 by Minoru Yamasaki.

↗ Brunswick Centre, London, England, UK, 1970 by Patrick Hodgkinson.

→ Sainte-Marie Lyon Day School, La Verpillière, France, 1976 by Georges Adilon.

↑ Hat Factory, Luckenwalde, Germany, 1923 by Erich
   Mendelsohn.

→ Ivar Aasen Centre, Ørsta, Norway, 2000
   by Sverre Fehn.

'Out of sorrow entire worlds have been built /
Out of longing great wonders have been willed'

— Nick Cave, '(Are You) The One
That I've Been Waiting For?'

↖ Simmons Hall, MIT, Cambridge, Massachusetts,
USA, 2002 by Steven Holl.
← Education Wing of the Cleveland Museum of Art,
Cleveland, Ohio, USA, 1971 by Marcel Breuer.

↑ Monument to Karl Liebknecht and Rosa Luxemburg,
Berlin, Germany, 1926 by Mies van der Rohe.

↑ Driving Range of the Asociación Paraguaya
De Golf (APG), Luque, Paraguay, 2013 by Javier
Corvalán + Laboratorio de Arquitectura.
↑ Webb Chapel Park Pavilion, Dallas, Texas, USA,
2012 by Studio Joseph.

↗ Biomedical Research Centre, Pamplona, Spain,
2011 by Vaíllo & Irigaray.
→ City of Orion, Plaine de Marha, Morocco, 2003
by Hannsjörg Voth.

'SHE REFERRED TO THE
HIGH-RISE AS IF IT WERE
SOME KIND OF HUGE ANIMATE
PRESENCE, BROODING
OVER THEM AND KEEPING
A MAGISTERIAL EYE ON THE
EVENTS TAKING PLACE.'

—

JG BALLARD

'The miracle of concrete music is ...
things begin to speak by themselves,
as if they were bringing a
message from a world unknown
to us and outside us.'

— Pierre Henri Marie Schaeffer

↖ Bangladesh National Capital Complex, Dhaka,
Bangladesh, 1983 by Louis Kahn.

↑ Maizières Music Conservatory, Maizieres-les-Metz,
France, 2009 by Dominique Coulon & Associés.

← Stone House / Interni Think Tank, Milan, Italy,
2010 by John Pawson.

↑ Valence Water Tower, Valence, France, 1971
by André Gomis and Tloupas Philolaos.

'A building is alive, like a man. Its integrity is to follow its own truth, its one single theme, and to serve its own single purpose.
A man doesn't borrow pieces of his body. A building doesn't borrow hunks of its soul.'

— Ayn Rand

↖ Buffalo City Court Building, Buffalo, New York,
   USA, 1974 by Pfohl, Roberts & Biggie.
← Wotruba Church, Vienna, Austria, 1976 by Fritz
   Wotruba and Fritz Gerhard Mayer.

↑ Sanctuary of Mary Queen of Peace Church,
   Neviges, Germany, 1973 by Gottfried Böhm.
→ Podčetrtek Traffic Circle, Podčetrtek, Slovenia,
   2012 by ENOTA.

↑ FamilYar, Kokkoni, Greece, 2008
by Workshop Dionisis Sotovikis.

↗ Maison du Brésil, Paris, France, 1959
by Le Corbusier.

151

'Brutalist architecture was a political
aesthetic, an attitude, a weapon,
dedicated to the precept that nothing was
too good for ordinary people.'

— Owen Hatherley

↑   Adan Martin Auditorio de Tenerife, Santa Cruz de
    Tenerife, Spain, 2003 by Santiago Calatrava.

→   National Theatre, London, England, UK, 1976
    by Denys Lasdun.

↖ Olivetti Administrative and Training Center,
Frankfurt am Main, Germany, 1972
by Egon Eiermann.
← Solo House, Cretas, Spain, 2012 by Pezo
von Ellrichshausen.

↑ Villa Shodhan, Ahmedabad, India, 1956
by Le Corbusier.
→ Johnson Museum of Art, Cornell University,
Ithaca, New York, USA, 1973 by
I. M. Pei & Partners.

'The brutalities of progress are
called revolutions. When they are over
we realize this: that the human
race has been roughly handled,
but that it has advanced.'

— Victor Hugo

← Monolith, Expo 02, Morat, Switzerland, 2002
by Ateliers Jean Nouvel and Gimm Architekten.

↑ Miami Marine Stadium, Miami, Florida, USA,
1963 by Hilario Candela.
→ Denge Sound Mirrors, Denge, Dungeness, Kent,
England, UK, late 1920s and early 1930s.

↑ Innovation Centre UC Anacleto Angelini, Santiago, Chile, 2014 by Alejandro Aravena / ELEMENTAL.
→ 4 x 4 House, Kobe, Japan, 2003 by Tadao Ando.

↗ New County Office and Court House Building, Goshen, New York, USA, 1963 by Paul Rudolph.

'Rudolph's work is pure, but the beauty
is in its austerity. There are no additions to
make it polite or cute. It is what it is.'

— Zaha Hadid

'Ah we wait till daylight hours /
Waiting for a sign from you /
Golden temples concrete towers'

— Simple Minds, 'Wall of Love'

← Avala Tower, Belgrade, Serbia, 1965
   by Uglješa Bogdanović and Slobodan Janjić.
↓ Metropolitan Cathedral of Christ the King,
   Liverpool, England, UK, 1967 by Frederick
   Gibberd.

→ Brasília TV tower, Brasília, Brazil, 1967
   by Lúcio Costa.

← SAS Royal Hotel, Copenhagen, Denmark, 1960 by Arne Jacobsen.
↙ Ruy Barbosa Labor Courthouse, São Paulo, Brazil, 2004 by Decio Tozzi.
↙ National Library of France, Paris, France, 1995 by DPA Dominique Perrault Architecture.

→ Knights of Columbus Headquarters, New Haven, Connecticut, USA, 1969 by Kevin Roche John Dinkeloo and Associates.
↓ KNSM Island Skydome, Amsterdam, The Netherlands, 1996 by Wiel Arets Architects.

↑ Torre Velasca, Milan, Italy, 1958 by BBPR.
↘ Shizuoka Press and Broadcasting Centre, Tokyo,
   Japan, 1967 by Kenzo Tange Associates.

↗ Torre Blancas, Madrid, Spain, 1969 by Francisco
   Javier Sáenz de Oiza.
→ Centre Point, London, England, UK, 1966
   by Richard Seifert and Partners.

'Now I'm in the subway and I'm looking for the flat / This one leads to this block, this one leads to that / The wind howls through the empty blocks looking for a home / I run through the empty stone because I'm all alone'

— The Clash, 'London's Burning'

↑ Stykkishólmur Church, Stykkishólmur, Iceland, 1990 by Jón Haraldsson.
← Gori Highway Rest Stops, Gori, Georgia, 2011 by Jürgen Mayer H. Architects.

→ Trans World Airlines (TWA) Terminal, JFK Airport, New York, New York, USA, 1962 by Eero Saarinen and Associates.

'THERE WAS
GOOD BRUTALISM AND BAD,
BUT EVEN THE BAD WAS DONE
IN EARNEST, IT TOOK
ITSELF SERIOUSLY, WHICH IS
A CRIME IN THE MARKET
WHOSE INSISTENCE
IS ON MINDLESS FUN AND
MORONIC FUN, JUST LOOK
AT TELEVISION.'

—

JONATHAN MEADES

← Villa Kogelhof, Kamperland, The Netherlands,
2013 by Paul de Ruiter Architects (previous pages).

↑ Geisel Library, University of California,
San Diego, California, USA, 1970 by William
Pereira & Associates.

→ Control Tower, Komazawa Olympic Park, Tokyo,
Japan, 1964 by Yoshinobu Ashihara.

'On the tenth floor, down the back stairs, it's a no man's land / Lights are flashing, cars are crashing, getting frequent now'

— Joy Division, 'Disorder'

↖ Landmarke Lausitzer Seenland, Senftenberg,
   Germany, 2008 by Stefan Giers Architektur
   & Landschaft.
← Pierresvives, Montpellier, France, 2012 by
   Zaha Hadid Architects.

↑ RW Concrete Church, Byeollae, South Korea,
   2013 by NAMELESS Architecture.
↗ Evans–DePass Residence, Fire Island, New York,
   USA, 1965 by Horace Gifford.
→ On the Cherry Blossom House, Tokyo, Japan,
   2008 by Junichi Sampei / ALX.

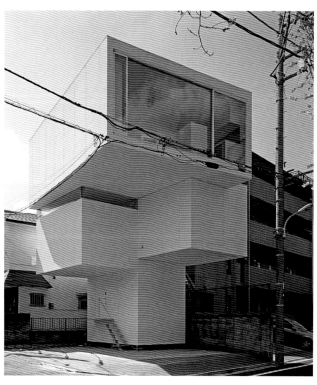

↑ SESC Pompéia Recreational Centre, São Paulo,
Brazil, 1977 by Lina Bo Bardi.

↗ Sainte-Marie-de-la-Tourette Convent, L'Abresle,
France, 1959 by Le Corbusier.

→ Southgate Estate, Runcorn New Town, England,
UK, 1977 by James Stirling.

'The play of light is everything, whether
it's in the films of Stanley Kubrick,
Ridley Scott and David Lynch, or the
architecture of Nicholas Hawksmoor,
Le Corbusier and Rem Koolhaas.'

— Jonathan Glancey

↑ Whitney Museum of American Art, New York,
New York, USA, 1966 by Marcel Breuer
and Associates.

→ Edificio Solimar, Havana, Cuba, 1944 by
Manuel Copado.

'I have always been attracted
to the voluptuousness of austerity.'

— Leonard Cohen

179

'It's an incredibly muscular use of concrete. It's not built, it's cast. You can't have something more like sculpture in architecture than [the Hayward Gallery].'

— Antony Gormley

← One Kemble Street (Space House), London, England, UK, 1968 by Richard Seifert & Partners.
↓ Spanish Cultural Heritage Institute, Madrid, Spain, 1988 by Fernando Higueras and Antonio Miró.

→ Hayward Gallery, South Bank Centre, London, England, UK, 1968 by Norman Engleback with John Attenborough, Warren Chalk, Dennis Crompton, Ron Herron and J. W. Szymaniak.

↑ Faculty of Architecture and Urbanism Building, University of São Paulo, Brazil, 1968 by João Batista Vilanova Artigas and Carlos Cascaldi.

→ Azuma Residence (Tower House), Tokyo, Japan, 1966 by Azuma Takamitsu.

'I am particularly fond of concrete, symbol of the construction progress of a whole century, submissive and strong as an elephant, monumental like stone, humble like brick.'

— Carlos Villanueva

↑   Wall House #2, Groningen, The Netherlands,
    2001 by John Hejduk.

→   Copan Building, São Paulo, Brazil, 1966
    by Oscar Niemeyer.

←   Druzhba Sanitarium, Kurpaty, Ukraine, 1985
    by Igor A. Vasilevsky.

↑   Hotel Sofitel Tokyo, Tokyo, Japan, 1994
    by Kiyonori Kikutake.

↗   Bierpinsel, Berlin, Germany, 1976 by Ralph
    Schüler and Ursulina Schüler-Witte.

↑ Place Picasso, Noisy-le-Grand, France, 1984
    by Manuel Núñez Yanowsky.
↗ Guangzhou Circle, Guangzhou, China, 2013
    by Joseph di Pasquale.

→ Electrabel Powerplant (Intercom), Monceau-sur-
    Sambre, Belgium, 1921.

← São Paulo Museum of Art, São Paulo, Brazil, 1968 by Lina Bo Bardi.
↓ Mendes da Rocha House (House in Butantã), São Paulo, Brazil, 1967 by Paulo Mendes da Rocha.

→ Säynätsalo Town Hall, Säynätsalo, Finland, 1952 by Alvar Aalto.

'I don't design nice buildings—I don't like them.
I like architecture to have some raw, vital, earthy quality.
You don't need to make concrete perfectly smooth
or paint it or polish it. If you consider changes in
the play of light on a building before it's built, you can
vary the colour and feel of concrete by daylight alone.'

— Zaha Hadid

← Marina City, Chicago, Illinois, USA, 1967
by Bertrand Goldberg.

→ Kivik Art Centre Pavilion, Österlen, Sweden, 2008
by David Chipperfield and Antony Gormley.
↓ City of Culture of Galicia, Santiago de Compostela,
Spain, 1999 by Eisenman Architects.

'GREY. IT MAKES NO STATEMENT WHATEVER; IT EVOKES NEITHER FEELINGS NOR ASSOCIATIONS; IT IS REALLY NEITHER VISIBLE NOR INVISIBLE. ITS INCONSPICUOUSNESS GIVES IT THE CAPACITY TO MEDIATE, TO MAKE VISIBLE, IN A POSITIVELY ILLUSIONISTIC WAY, LIKE A PHOTOGRAPH. IT HAS THE CAPACITY THAT NO OTHER COLOUR HAS, TO MAKE 'NOTHING' VISIBLE.'

—

GERHARD RICHTER

'The Beautiful is always strange ... it always contains a touch of strangeness, of simple, unpremeditated and unconscious strangeness, and it is that touch of strangeness that gives it its particular quality as Beauty.'

— Charles Baudelaire

↑   Les Choux de Créteil, Créteil, France, 1974
    by Gérard Grandval.

→   Border Checkpoint, Sarpi, Georgia, 2011
    by J. Mayer H. Architects.

← Kagawa Prefectural Government Office, Kagawa Prefecture, Japan, 1958 by Kenzo Tange.
↓ Tribunal de Contas, São Paulo, Brazil, 1971 by Aflalo / Gasperini Architects.

→ Lyndon Baines Johnson (LBJ) Presidential Library, Austin, Texas, USA, 1971 by Gordon Bunschaft, Skidmore, Owings and Merrill (SOM).
↘ Jefferson Hall, East-West Center, Honolulu, Hawaii, USA, 1963 by I. M. Pei.

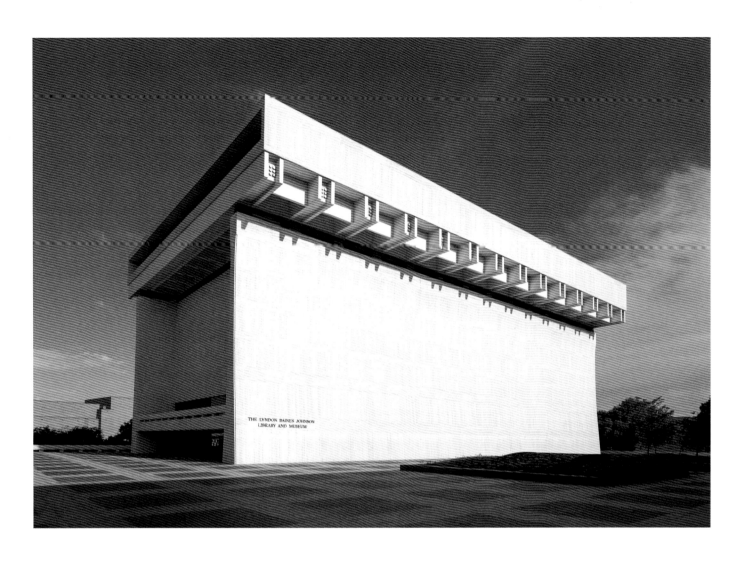

'The secret is not in seeking new landscapes, but in having new eyes.'

— Marcel Proust

← Salk Institute, La Jolla, California, USA, 1965 by Louis Kahn.

↖ Waste to Energy Plant, Roskilde, Denmark, 2014 by
    Erick van Egeraat.
← España Library, Santo Domingo, Colombia, 2005
    by Giancarlo Mazzanti.

↗ Chienbergreben House, Gelterkinden, Switzerland,
    2012 by Buchner Bründler Architekten.
↑ Valleaceron Chapel, Ciudad Real, Spain, 2000
    by Sancho-Madridejos Architecture Office.
→ Concert Hall, Blaibach, Germany, 2014 by Peter
    Haimerl Architektur.

↑ Endo Pharmaceutical Laboratories, Garden City,
   New York, USA, 1964 by Paul Rudolph.

→ Shakespeare Tower, Barbican Estate, London,
   England, UK, 1976 by Chamberlin, Powell and Bon.
↗ New Dehli Municipal Council Building, New Delhi,
   India, 1983 by Kuldip Singh.

← Central Research and Design Institute for Robotics
  and Technical Cybernetics, Saint Petersburg,
  Russia, 1987 by S. V. Savin and B. I. Artiushin.
↓ Qatar University, Doha, Qatar, 2013 by Kamal
  El-Kafrawi.

→ Sardar Vallabhbhai Patel Stadium, Ahmedabad,
  India, 1960 by Charles Correa Associates.
→ Chapel of the Holy Cross, Sedona, Arizona,
  USA, 1956 by Richard Hein and August K. Strotz.
↘ Museum of Anthropology, Universtiy of
  British Columbia, Vancouver, Canada, 1978
  by Arthur Erickson.

↑ Gymnasium, Mülimatt, Switzerland, 2010 by
   Studio Vacchini Architetti with Paul Zimmermann
   and Jerôme Wolfensberger.
→ Autobahn Church Siegerland, Wilnsdorf, Germany,
   2013 by Schneider + Schumacher.

↑ Universita Luigi Bocconi, Milan, Italy, 2008
   by Grafton Architects.

↗ Ulster Museum, Belfast, Northern Ireland,
   UK, 1972 by Francis Pym.
→ La Congiunta Museum, Giornico,
   Switzerland, 1992 by Peter Märkli.

'Architecture is the will
of an epoch translated
into space.'

— Mies van der Rohe

↖ Le Point Zéro, La Grande-Motte, France,
1967 by Jean Balladur.
← Welbeck Street Car Park, London, England,
UK, 1970 by Michael Blampied and Partners.

↑ Holy Redeemer Church, Tenerife, Spain,
2007 by Fernando Menis.
→ Faculty of Art and Architecture Building, Yale
University, New Haven, Connecticut, USA,
1964 by Paul Rudolph.

'Ugliness is, in a way, superior to beauty because it lasts.'

— Serge Gainsbourg

← Interdesign Building, Beirut, Lebanon, 1997 by Khalil Khoury.
↓ Casa do Cinema Manoel de Oliveira, Porto, Portugal, 2003 by Eduardo Souto de Moura.

→ Saint Mary's Cathedral, Tokyo, Japan, 1964 by Kenzo Tange Associates.
↘ Energiebunker Wilhelmsburg, Hamburg, Germany, 2015 by Hegger Hegger Schleiff.

216

← Crematorium Heimolen, Sint-Niklaas, Belgium,
  2008 by Claus en Kaan Architecten.
↙ Sean O'Casey Community Centre, Dublin, Republic
  of Ireland, 2008 by O'Donnell+Tuomey.

→ Titan / Kubus Extension, Bern Historical Museum,
  Bern, Switzerland, 2009 by :mlzd.
↓ The Wall of Nishihara House, Tokyo, Japan, 2013
  by SabaoArch.

'There are no beautiful surfaces
without a terrible depth.'

— Friedrich Nietzsche

↑ Cidade das Artes, Rio de Janeiro, Brazil, 2013 by Christian de Portzamparc.
← La Merced Market, Mexico City, Mexico, 1957 by Enrique del Moral.

↗ College Life Insurance Company of America, Indianapolis, Indiana, USA, 1971 by Kevin Roche John Dinkeloo and Associates.
↗ Gunma Music Centre, Takasaki, Gunma Prefecture, Japan, 1961 by Antonin Raymond.
→ De Ark Church, Schaesberg, The Netherlands, 1967 by Peter Sigmond.

Quotations

Adjaye, David (b.1966), London-based, Tanzanian-born architect, whose influences range from contemporary art, music and science to African art forms and the civic life of cities.
— Page 133. From the BBC2 series *Class Clips* in which architect David Adjaye defends the Tricorn Centre – a well-known example of Brutalist architecture in England that was demolished in 2004. In 2001 it was voted by BBC Radio 4 listeners as the most hated building in the UK.

American Psycho
— Page 124. American-Canadian film released in 2000 with screenplay by Mary Harron (b.1953) and Guinevere Turner (b.1968) based on Bret Easton Ellis' (b.1964) transgressive postmodern novel *American Psycho* (published in 1991 by Vintage Books) featuring protagonist Patrick Bateman, a Manhattan businessman and serial killer.

Auden, W H (1907–1973), British-born poet known for his engagement with political and social themes.
— Page 126. Excerpt from the poem 'Petition' in *The Collected Poetry of W. H. Auden* first published by Random House in 1945.

Ballard, JG (1930–2009), British novelist, short story writer, and essayist.
— Page 57. Ballard's novel *High Rise* takes place in an ultra-modern, 40-storey high-rise building in which, over the course of three months, the 2,000 residents descend from civilisation to tribalism to hunter-gatherer savagery. *High Rise* was first published by Jonathan Cape in 1975.
— Page 143. Also from *High Rise*.

Banham, Reyner (1922–1988), Influential British critic who wrote primarily on the subjects of architecture, design and popular culture.
— Page 36. 'The New Brutalism', first published in *The Architectural Review* in December 1955 and subsequently in his 1966 book *The New Brutalism: Ethic or Aesthetic?* In this seminal essay architectural critic Reyner Banham attempted to codify the then emerging architectural movement of Brutalism.
— Page 39. Also from 'The New Brutalism'.
— Page 103. Also from 'The New Brutalism'.

Banksy, English graffiti artist, political activist and film director whose real identity is unknown.
— Page 50. Quoted in an online article by Australian architect Steve Rose, 'Banksy on Architecture' (29 October 2013) in which Rose critiques Banksy's position on the new One World Trade Centre building in New York. Banksy's opinion was published in *The New York Times* on 27 October 2013 under the title 'The biggest eyesore in New York is not the graffiti, argues Banksy, it's under construction at ground zero'.

Baudelaire, Charles (1821–1867), French poet, essayist, art critic and pioneering translator of Edgar Allan Poe, best known for his collection of poetry *Les Fleurs du Mal*.
— Page 196. Baudelaire's definition of modern beauty sprang from a discussion of Ingres' nudes at the 1855 Exposition Universelle in Paris.

Becher, Hilla (1934–2015), German conceptual artist and photographer who worked in a collaborative partnership with Bernd Becher.
— Page 122. Hilla Becher, speaking a year after the death of her husband Bernd Becher, was interviewed by Tobias Haberl and Dominik Wichmann for *Süddeutsche Zeitung Magazin*, 2008.

Blur, English rock band, formed in London in 1988. The group consists of singer-keyboardist Damon Albarn (b.1968), guitarist-singer Graham Coxon (b.1969), bassist Alex James (b.1968) and drummer Dave Rowntree (b.1964).
— Page 118. Lyric from 'New World Towers' on the album *The Magic Whip*, released by Parlophone and Warner Bros Records in 2015. Written by Steven James, David Rowntree, Damon Albarn and Graham Coxon. © Wixen Music Uk Ltd, Emi Music Publishing Ltd, Warner/Chappell Music Ltd.

Bowie, David (b.1947), British singer, songwriter, record producer, painter and actor, known for his multiple incarnations including Ziggy Stardust.
— Page 65. Lyric from 'Thru These Architect's Eyes' from the album *Outside*, released in 1995 by Virgin. Written by David Bowie, Reeves Gabrels and David Robert Jones. © Strept Throat Music, Tintoretto Music.

Breton, André (1896–1966), French writer, poet, anarchist and anti-fascist, best known as the founder of Surrealism.
— Page 99. The last sentence of Bréton's book *Nadja*, published in 1928 by Grove Press, one of the iconic works of the French Surrealist movement.

Cave, Nick (b.1957), Australian-born musician, songwriter, author, screenwriter and composer best known as the frontman of the band Nick Cave and the Bad Seeds.
— Page 136. Lyric from 'Are You The One That I've Been Waiting For?' on the album *The Boatman's Call* released by Mute/Reprise in 1997. Written by Nick Cave. © Embassy Music Corp. O/B/o Mute Song

Chandler, Raymond 1888–1959, American-born novelist and writer of crime fiction featuring the private detective Philip Marlowe.
— Page 46. From Chandler's crime novel *The Big Sleep*, first published in 1939 by AA Knopf.

Cohen, Leonard (b 1934), Prolific Canadian singer-songwriter, musician, painter, poet and novelist.
— Page 40. Lyric from 'Anthem', a track featured on the album *The Future*, released by Columbia in 1992. Written by Mike Strange and Leonard Cohen. © Sony/ATV Songs LLC.
— Page 178. Radio interview for *Variety Tonight*, CBC (Canada). Interviewed by Vicki Gabereau, Cohen commented on his simple lifestyle. Excerpt from *Leonard Cohen on Leonard Cohen: Interviews and Encounters* edited by Jeff Burger, published by Chicago Review Press in 2014.

Eisenman, Peter (b.1932), American architect and educator particularly known for his large-scale housing and urban design projects as well as for the 'Memorial to the Murdered Jews of Europe' in Berlin.
— Page 114. Peter Eisenman in conversation with Robert Ivy, during an interview entitled 'Challenging Norms: Eisenman's obsession' for *Architectural Record*, October 2003.

Gainsbourg, Serge (1928–1991), French singer-songwriter widely regarded as one of the most important figures in French popular music.
— Page 214. Quoted by Stephen Bayley in *The Telegraph* article 'Why beauty is rarely worth it' on 26 October 2012.

Gehry, Frank (b.1929), Canadian-American contemporary architect, one of the most influential of his generation, winner of the Pritzker Prize and the RIBA Gold Medal.
— Page 63. The quote featured in the book *Home (Chic Simple)* by Julie Iovine, Maria Robledo and Kim Johnson Gross, published by Knopf in 1993.

Glancey, Jonathan (b.1954), Architecture critic, writer and correspondent for *The Guardian* newspaper in the UK.
— Page 176. Glancey in an article titled 'From Metropolis to Blade Runner: architecture that stole the show', about films in which buildings take a starring role. Published in *The Guardian* 5 November 2009.

Glass, Philip (b.1937), American composer known for his operas, symphonies, minimalist compositions and wide-ranging creative collaborations.
— Page 78. From an interview in *Glass, A Portrait of Philip in Twelve Parts*, a 2007 film documentary directed by Scott Hicks about Glass' life and work.

Gormley, Antony (b.1950), British sculptor.
— Page 180. Published in www.bdonline.co.uk on 10 July 2008 in the article 'Experts enthuse over the Hayward 40 years on', in which the Hayward Gallery invited a panel of experts to muse on the building's great achievements and what it means to them as part of the 40th anniversary of the Hayward's opening.

Grass, Günter (1927–2015), German novelist, poet, playwright, artist and recipient of the 1999 Nobel Prize in Literature.
— Page 84. *The Tin Drum* is the first book of Grass's Danzig Trilogy and is recognized as one of the most important German novels of the post-war era. The book was first published by Hermann Luchterhand Verlag in 1959.

Hadid, Zaha (b.1944), Iraqi-British architect and recipient of the Pritzker Architecture Prize and the AIA Gold Medal.
— Page 23. Zaha Hadid interviewed by Blake Godnik for *Newsweek* for the article 'Design Diva Hits a High Z: Zaha Hadid', published on 21 September 2011.
— Page 159. Zaha Hadid's contribution to Alexandra Lange's article 'Seven Leading Architects Defend the World's Most Hated Buildings', in which the architects were challenged to defend seven of the world's 'most hated buildings'. Hadid's comments on Paul Rudolph's Orange County Government Center in Goshen County, New York, was published in *The New York Times Style Magazine* on 5 June 2015.
— Page 191. Zaha Hadid in conversation with Jonathan Glancey for *The Guardian*. The interview, 'I Don't Do Nice', published on 9 October 2006, took place after her first work in the UK had been unveiled.

Hatherley, Owen (b.1981), British writer and journalist whose works on architecture include *Militant Modernism*.
— Page 96. From Hatherley's book *Militant Modernism*, in which he argues for a Modernism of everyday life, immersed in questions of socialism, sexual politics and technology. Published by Zero Books in 2009.
— Page 152. From an article in *The Guardian* titled 'Penthouse and pavement' in which Hatherley discusses English Heritage's regeneration of Park Hill Estate in Sheffield, Britain's largest example of Brutalist architecture. Published 2 May 2009.

Hugo, Victor (1802–1885), French novelist, poet and dramatist whose works include *Les Misérables* and *Notre-Dame de Paris*.
— Page 156. From Victor Hugo's historical novel *Les Misérables*, first published in 1862 and widely considered one of the greatest literary works of the nineteenth century.

Johnson, Philip (1906–2005), American architect known for his promotion of the International Style and his role founding the department of architecture and design at the Museum of Modern Art in New York in 1930.
— Page 20. Quoted in Paul Goldberger's obituary for Philip Johnson published in *The New York Times* on 27 January 2005.

Joy Division, English post-punk band formed in Manchester in 1976 with singer Ian Curtis (1956–1980), guitarist and keyboardist Bernard Sumner (b.1956), bassist Peter Hook (1956–) and drummer Stephen Morris (b.1957).
— Page 174. Lyric from 'Disorder' on *Unknown Pleasures*, Joy Division's debut album released by Factory Records in 1979. Written by Bernard Sumner, Peter Hook, Ian Curtis and Stephen Morris. © Universal Music Publishing Ltd.

Le Corbusier (1887–1965), Pioneering Swiss-born French architect who coined the term *béton brut* (raw concrete) and whose influential Brutalist buildings include Ronchamp Chapel and the Unité d'Habitation in France and Chandigargh in India.
— Page 92. So reads an inscription on a sidewalk in Battery Park City, New York. Le Corbusier visited the city for the first time in 1935 and was quoted in *The New York Herald Tribune* in August 1961, according to writer Valeria Luiselli in her article 'Collected Poems' published in *The New Yorker* on 9 December 2014.

Locke (2013), Critically acclaimed British film written and directed by Steven Knight (b.1959) starring Tom Hardy (b.1977) as Ivan Locke.
— Page 91. The day before he must supervise a large concrete pour in Birmingham, construction foreman Ivan Locke engages in a series of phone calls, a number of which are with his colleague, Donal to ensure the pour is successful. The entire film takes place at night, in a car, while Locke drives from Birmingham to London.

Mayne, Thom (b.1944), American architect, founder of SCI-Arc (Southern California Institute of Architecture) and principal of the influential Los Angeles-based architecture practice Morphosis.
— Page 54. Thom Mayne, quoted in David Wharton's article 'Arts Park Theater Design Poses a Major Risk: Striking design alienates environmentalists, but brings panache to project in search of artistic credibility' for the *Los Angeles Times*, in June 1989, on the proposals from Mayne's firm Morphosis to build the theatre for Arts Park LA.

Meades, Jonathan (b.1947), British writer, journalist, essayist and film-maker known for his BBC architecture documentaries.
— Page 25. Published on design blog Dezeen on 15 September 2014 in an article about Brutalism with the title 'There was good brutalism and bad, but even the bad was done in earnest'.
— Page 134. Also from 'There was good brutalism and bad, but even the bad was done in earnest'.
— Page 169. Also from 'There was good brutalism and bad, but even the bad was done in earnest'.

Moholy-Nagy, László (1895–1946), Hungarian painter, photographer and professor at the influential Bauhaus school in Weimar.
— Page 44. First published as the caption to one of Moholy-Nagy's photogram experiments in his book of 1925, *Malerei, Photographie, Film* (Painting, Photography, Film), and subsequently in the book *In Focus: Laszlo Moholy-Nagy: Photographs from the J.Paul Getty Museum*, first published by Getty Publications in 1995.

Nietzsche, Friedrich (1844–1900), German philosopher, cultural critic, poet and Latin and Greek scholar.
— Page 217. Nietzsche's statement was a response to Greek art, and has been attributed to a discarded draft of the foreword to his book on German composer Richard Wagner, *Der Fall Wagner* (The Case of Wagner) originally published in 1888.

Orwell, George (1903–1950), English novelist, essayist, journalist and critic.
— Page 13. The Ministry of Truth is a government department in Airstrip One (formerly known as Great Britain) which is responsible for propaganda and historical revisionism. The building is part of both the physical and psychological dystopian landscape in Orwell's classic novel *Nineteen Eighty-Four*, first published in 1949 by Secker & Warburg.

Proust, Marcel (1871–1922), French novelist, critic, and essayist best known for his monumental seven-part novel *À la recherche du temps perdu* (In Search of Lost Time).
— Page 201. Excerpt from 'La Prisonnière', the fifth volume of *À la recherche du temps perdu* (In Search of Lost Time) originally published by Grasset and Gallimard in 1913.

Pulp, English rock band formed in Sheffield in 1978 and fronted by vocalist Jarvis Cocker.
— Page 69. Lyric from 'Sheffield: Sex City' on the album *Intro - The Gift Recordings*, released by Island in 1993. Written by Jarvis Cocker, Russell Senior, Stephen Mackey, Candida Doyle and Nick Banks. © Island Music Ltd.

Rand, Ayn (1905–1982), Russian-born American novelist, philosopher, playwrite and screenwriter.
— Page 71. Quote by the architect protagonist Howard Roark in Ayn Rand's *The Fountainhead* (first published in 1943 by Bobbs Merrill). Roark is an individualistic architect who chooses to struggle in obscurity rather than compromise his artistic vision. The character of Roark was at least partly inspired by the American architect Frank Lloyd Wright.
— Page 87. Also said by Howard Roark in *The Fountainhead*.
— Page 148. Also said by Howard Roark in *The Fountainhead*.

Richter, Gerhard (1932–), German visual artist and one of the pioneers of the New European Painting.
— Page 195. From a letter written in 1975 by Gerhard Richter to Edy de Wilde, the director of the Stedelijk Museum in Amsterdam, and subsequently included in *Gerhard Richter: Text, Writings, Interviews and Letters 1961-2007* published by Thames & Hudson in 2009.

Rohan, Timothy, Architectural historian whose research focuses on Modernism.
— Page 17. Excerpt from Rohan's article, 'The Rise and Fall of Brutalism, Rudolph and the Liberal Consensus' featured in the book *CLOG: Brutalism, an anthology of writings on Brutalism* published by Clog 2013.

Ruskin, John (1819–1900), Leading art critic of the Victorian era and prominent social thinker and philanthropist.
— Page 89. Excerpt from the chapter 'On the Nature of Gothic' in *The Stones of Venice*, first published in 1851, Ruskin's three-volume treatise on Venetian art and architecture.

Saint Etienne, English dance-pop band, formed in 1990 in London, consisting of members Sarah Cracknell (b.1967), Bob Stanley (b.1964) and Pete Wiggs (b.1966).
— Page 48. Lyric from the track 'When I Was Seventeen', which featured on the album *Words and Music by Saint Etienne*, released by Heavenly / Universal UMC in 2012. Written by Peter Wiggs, Sarah Cracknell and Bob Stanley. © Kobalt Music Services Ltd. Kms

Schaeffer, Pierre Henri Marie (1910–1995), French composer, writer, broadcaster and media theorist, known as the inventor of *musique concrète*, a style of electronic music.
— Page 144. From *À la recherche d'une musique concrète* (In Search of a Concrete Music) originally published by Éditions du Seuil in 1952.

Self, Jack (b.1987), Architect and writer based in London, director of the REAL foundation.
— Page 66. In his essay 'The Morality of Concrete', Jack Self contends that Brutalism has its roots in state-led reconstruction after World War II. The essay featured in the book *CLOG: Brutalism, an anthology of writings on Brutalism* published by Clog in 2013.

Simple Minds, Scottish rock band formed in 1977 by Jim Kerr (b.1959) and Charlie Burchill (b.1959).
— Page 160. Lyric from 'Wall Of Love' on Simple Mind's album *Street Fighting Years*, released in 1989 by Virgin Records / A&M Records. Written by Jim Kerr, Charles Burchill and Michael Macneil. © Sony/ATV Music Publishing LLC.

Smithson, Alison and Peter. Alison Smithson (1928–1993). Peter Smithson (1923–2003). English architects, closely associated with the New Brutalism movement.
— Page 117. Quoted in Reyner Banham's article 'The New Brutalism', first published in *The Architectural Review* in December 1955 and subsequently in Banham's 1966 book *The New Brutalism: Ethic or Aesthetic?* In this seminal essay architectural critic Reyner Banham attempted to codify the then emerging architectural movement of Brutalism.

Stella, Frank (b.1936), American-born painter whose work is associated with Minimalism and Post-Painterly Abstraction.
— Page 74. Frank Stella quoted in *Frank Stella at Two Thousand: Changing the Rules*, by Bonnie Clearwater and published by the Museum of Contemporary Art in 2000.

Suede, English alternative rock band formed in London in 1989 by singer Brett Anderson (b.1967), guitarist Richard Oakes (b.1976), bass player Mat Osman (b.1967), drummer Simon Gilbert (b.1965) and keyboardist / rhythm guitarist Neil Codling (b.1973).
— Page 130. Lyric from 'Stay Together', a non-album single released in 1994 on Nude Records. Written by Brett Anderson and Bernard Butler. © Kobalt Music Services Ltd. Kms, Polygram Music Publishing Ltd. Gb, Stage Three Music Ltd.

Tange, Kenzo (1913–2005), Japanese architect and urban planner, and winner of the 1987 Pritzker Architecture Prize.
— Page 18. From Kenzo Tange's acceptance speech when he was awarded the Pritzker Architecture Prize in 1987.

The Clash, English punk rock band formed in 1976 fronted by vocalist Joe Strummer (1952–2002).
— Page 165. Lyric fom the track 'London's Burning', released on The Clash's eponymous debut album in 1977. Written by Topper Headon, Mick Jones, Joe Strummer and Paul Simonon. © Nineden Ltd.

The Human League, English electronic new wave band formed in Sheffield in 1977 by Phil Oakey (b.1955), Joanne Catherall (b.1962) and Susanne Sulley (b.1963).
— Page 83. Lyric from the track 'Blind Youth' on the album *Reproduction* released by Virgin in 1979. Written by Marsh, Oakey, Ware. © BMG Rights Management US, LLC.

The Jam, English punk rock and Mod revival band formed in 1972 fronted by vocalist and songwriter Paul Weller (b.1958).
— Page 100. Lyric from 'That's Entertainment' featured on the The Jam's 1980 album *Sound Affects* (Polydor). Written by Arthur Schwartz and Howard Dietz. © Chappell & Co. Inc.

Underworld, British electronic group formed in 1980 in Cardiff by Karl Hyde (b.1957) and Rick Smith (b.1959).
Page 31. Lyric from the 1993 single, 'Mmm...Skyscraper I Love You' on the album *dubnobasswithmyheadman* released in 1994 by Junior Boy's Own. The song's title derives from an art compilation by Underworld's design company, Tomato. © 1993 London.

van der Rohe, Mies (1886–1969), German-born architect who helped define Modernist architecture in both Europe and the USA in the early and mid-twentieth century.
— Page 213. From Mies van der Rohe's 1924 text 'Architecture and the Times'. Translated from the German by Philip Johnson and published by the Museum of Modern Art, New York in 1947 in *Mies van der Rohe*.

Villanueva, Carlos (1900–1975), Venezuelan Modernist architect.
— Page 182. Widely attributed to Villanueva in various sources.

Wainwright, Oliver, British architecture and design critic for the *The Guardian* newspaper.
— Page 94. Wainwright in an article titled 'Why Arthur Scargill is reluctant to leave his £1.5m Barbican flat' about the high cost of real estate in the increasingly popular Brutalist building 'The Barbican in London. Published in *The Guardian* on 7 October 2012.

Picture Credits

Every reasonable attempt has been made to identify owners of copyright.
Errors and omissions notified to the publisher will be corrected in subsequent editions.

Abbreviations are: R – right, L – left, T – top, B – bottom, C – centre, TR – top right,
TL – top left, BR – bottom right, BL – bottom left.

age fotostock 164T | age fotostock/View Pictures 139 | age fotostock/© Peter Cook 107 | age fotostock/© Schütze/Rodemann 174T | akg-images 76TL | akg-images / Album / Oronoz 180B | akg-images / Paul Almasy 212T | akg-images / Rainer Hackenberg 148B | akg-images / Schütze / Rodemann 62T, 111R, 177T | akg-images / ullstein bild / ullstein - Hechtenberg / Caro 155T | akg-images / VIEW Pictures / Sue Barr 8R | Alex Rainer 98T | Arcaid Images / Alamy Stock Photo 60 | Architectenbureau Paul de Ruiter bv 190B | Architectural Press Archive / RIBA Collections 11L, 114T, 115T, 125, 135, 68 | Architectures Jean Nouvel & GIMM Architekten, associated architect. Photos : Philippe Ruault 156 | Archives of the Cleveland Museum of Art 138B | Arnold Paira/laif/Camera Press 32 | Azuma Architect 183 | Beinecke Rare Book and Manuscript Library 44 | Ben Schnall, photographer. Marcel Breuer papers. Archives of American Art, Smithsonian Institution 46T | John S Lander/LightRocket via Getty Images 70T | Broekbakema, Menno Emmink 102T | Carol M Highsmith's America, Library of Congress, Prints and Photographs Division 207TR | Chicago History Museum 35R | Courtesy Arieh Sharon and Eldar Sharon 76B | Courtesy Fondation Le Corbusier 120 | Courtesy Kevin Roche John Dinkeloo and Associates LLC 219TL | Courtesy Mark Hackett 211T | Courtesy of Joseph Di Pasquale 188R | Courtesy Pezo von Ellrichshausen 127T, 154B | Courtesy Yorgo Tloupas 147 | Courtesy Zvi Hecker 77B | De Beeldunie / Freek van Arkel 102B | Didier Faustino 2005/ © ADAGP/Photo Wansoon Park 53BR | Dreamstime 27B | Edmund Sumner/ARTUR IMAGES 22T | Ezra Stoller © Esto. 17, 72, 124, 198T | Facundo de Zuviria 26 | Floto + Warner/OTTO 130 | Geisel Library, Robert Glasheen Collection, Special Collections & Archives, University of California, San Diego 172 | Getty Images 7R, 8L, 11R, 33, 36, 47R, 47L, 69, 106, 153, 165T, 165B, 192, 212B | Horace Gifford/courtesy Chris Rawlins 175TR | J. MAYER H. / Jesko M. Johnsson-Zahn 166B, 197 | James Ewing/OTTO, 155B | James Morris/VIEW/ARTUR IMAGES 9R | John Donat / RIBA Collections 11C, 206B | John Maltby / RIBA Collections 180T, 205L | John S Lander/LightRocket via Getty Images 70T | Kevin Roche John Dinkeloo and Associates LLC 163R | KEYSTONE/Str 61B | Krzysztof Dydynski / Lonely Planet Images / Getty Images 56B | LEHITKUVA / Markku Ulander 122L | Magda Biernat/OTTO 21 | MAISANT Ludovic / Hemis.fr / SuperStock 76 TR | Matthew Ziemba - In affiliation with DiDonato Associates 55 | Michael Portman, The AmericasMart 3 Collection, The Portman Archives, LLC 103R | Mischa Keijser/De Beeldunie 219B | Paul Warchol 162TL | Peter Bennetts 78B, 87T | Peter Miller 81B | Photo Addison Godel 16 | Photo Arjen Schmitz 81T | Photo by Guillermo Zamora. Courtesy of Sordo Madaleno Arquitectos 114B | Photo by View Pictures/UIG via Getty Images 164B | Photo Carlo Fumarola 207TL | Photo Cemal Emden 151 | Photo copyright Eli Golan / Courtesy Dani Karavan 78T | Photo courtesy Bunker Arquitectura 98B | Photo courtesy Dionisis Sotovikis 150 | Photo courtesy Fernando Menis 213T | Photo courtesy Geoffrey Goldberg 29 | Photo courtesy Otxotorena Arquitectos 86T | Photo courtesy Vaillo Irigaray 141T | Photo Darren Bradley 35L, 122R | Photo David Bleeker 184 | Photo David Cabrera 43 | Photo Earl Carter/courtesy Sean Godsell Architect 74T | Photo Eduard Hueber 140B | Photo Edward Beierle 203BR | Photo Fernando Guerra and Sérgio Guerra/courtesy Barbosa & Guimarães 23 | Photo Fran Parente 97 | Photo Frédéric Chaubin 61T, 186, 206T | Photo Gerry Johansson 193R | Photo Gubbins Arquitectos 80T | Photo Hannes Henz 54L | Photo Helene Binet 42 | Photo Henry Hutter/Courtesy Zvi Hecker 77TL | Photo Hufton and Crow/Courtesy Heatherwick Studio 46B | Photo Iain Jacques 56T | Photo Iwan Baan 110B, 118 | Photo James Burns 196 | Photo Jan Bitter 163L | Photo Leonardo Finotti 140T | Photo Margherita Spiluttini, © Architekturzentrum Wien, Collection 211B | Photo Mikel Muruzabal 94L, 152 | Photo Miran Kambic/courtesy ENOTA 149B | Photo Museo di arte moderna e contemporanea di Trento e Rovereto 28L | Photo Neutelings Riedijk Architecten 25B | Photo Nicolás Saieh 158L | Photo Peter Franc 189 | Photo Pieter Kers/Courtesy Rudy Uytenhaak 67 | Photo Rasmus Norlander 85 | Photo Reiulf Ramstad Arkitekter AS 121B | Photo Rob 't Hart/ Courtesy MVRDV 95T | Photo Roberto Conte 104 | Photo Roland Halbe 28R, 45T, 99B, 203BL | Photo Ruedi Walti 203T | Photo Scala, Florence 59B, 126 | Photo Sergio Gomez/Courtesy Correo Publicaciones 88B | Photo Vib Architecture 112T | Photo © Eugeni Pons / courtesy Dominique Coulon & associés 145 | Photo © NAMELESS Architecture 175TL | Photo © Tim Van de Velde/courtesy Erick van Egeraat 202T | Photo: Helge Hansen/Hydro 34TL | Photo: Vik Pahwa (www.vikpahwa.com) 148T | Photograph courtesy: Madan Mahatta and Photoink 205R | RCAHMS (Alexander Buchanan Campbell Collection. Photographer: G Forrest Wilson) 58B | RCAHMS (Sir Basil Spence Archive) 132 | Riba Collections 10L, 57, 80, 101, 133B, 133T, 218B | Richard Einzig / arcaidimages.com 177 | Robert Harding Picture Library Ltd / Alamy Stock Photo160B | Roberto Conte facebook.com/ilcontephotography 135B | saai | Südwestdeutsches Archiv für Architektur und Ingenieurbau, Karlsruher Institut für Technologie, Werkarchiv Egon Eiermann/photo Horstheinz Neuendorff 154T | saai | Südwestdeutsches Archiv für Architektur und Ingenieurbau, Karlsruher Institut für Technologie, Werkarchiv Egon Eiermann/photo Reinhard Friedrich 93 | Shutterstock 108B | Stefan Dauth/ARTUR IMAGES 52 | Stefan Müller-Naumann/ ARTUR IMAGES 113 | Süddeutsche Zeitung Photo / Alamy Stock Photo 187R | Ty Cole/OTTO 213B, 159 | Unidentified photographer. Marcel Breuer Papers, 1920-1986. Archives of American Art, Smithsonian Institution 84 | © AKTC-AKAA/Courtesy of architect/D. Mikhaylov (photographer) 59T | © Arco Images GmbH / Alamy Stock Photo 188L | © Axel Hartmann/ ARTUR IMAGES 95B | © Barbara Staubach/ARTUR IMAGES 176, 190T | © Benjamin Antony Monn/ARTUR IMAGES 200 | © Bettmann/CORBIS 178 | © Bildarchiv Foto Marburg 136 | © Bontinck Architecture & Engineering 27T | © Christian Richters 88T, 94R, 216T | © Collection Artedia/Parent Claude Virilio Paul /Artedia/Leemage Publicite soumise a autorisation prealable 137 | © Geurt Besselink/agefotostock 36L | © Gunter Marx Photography/CORBIS 207B | © Hemis / Alamy Stock Photo 70B, 162B | © Heritage Image Partnership Ltd / Alamy Stock Photo 10R | © imageBROKER / Alamy Stock Photo 161 | © Inigo Bujedo Aguirre/VIEW/ARTUR IMAGES 193L | © Irina Opachevsky | dreamstime.com 41 | © Jan Kempenaers 19, 123 | © Klaus Frahm/ARTUR IMAGES 75 | © Lars Gruber/ARTUR IMAGES 87B | © Marcus Bredt/ ARTUR IMAGES 129 | © Mark Wohlrab/ARTUR IMAGES 209 | © mastix / Alamy Stock Photo 24B | © Matteo Rossi/ARTUR IMAGES 131 | © Michael Jantzen 74B | © MIT Libraries, Rotch Visual Collections, courtesy of Peter Serenyi 31L | © Mona Zamdmer 92 | © Monheim: Florian/ Arcaid/Corbis 45B | © Neil Setchfield / Alamy Stock Photo 187L | © Pascal Lemaître/Breuer Marcel/Artedia/Leemage 10L, 99T | © Patrick McArdle / Alamy Stock Photo 9L | © Paul Riddle/ VIEW/ARTUR IMAGES 174B | © Peter Jordan_NE / Alamy Stock Photo 7L | © Robert Schlesinger/dpa/Corbis 115B | © Roberto Esposti / Alamy Stock Photo 30 | © Roland Halbe 14, 100, 127B | © Sven Otte/ARTUR IMAGES 166T | © The Art Archive / Alamy 110T | © the artist Hannsjörg Voth/photo Ingrid Amslinger 141B | © Timo Klein/ARTUR IMAGES 217T | © Walter Bibikow / age fotostock 71BR | © Wayne Andrews/Esto. 204 | © William Edwards / Alamy Stock Photo 66 | ©AP/PA Images 83B | ©Hufton+Crow 71BL, 218T

Phaidon Press Limited
Regent's Wharf
All Saints Street
London N1 9PA

Phaidon Press Inc.
65 Bleecker Street
New York, NY 10012

phaidon.com

First published 2016
Reprinted 2017 (twice), 2018, 2019
© 2016 Phaidon Press Limited

ISBN 978 0 7148 7108 0

A CIP catalogue record for this book is available from the British Library and the Library of Congress.

Commissioning Editor: Virginia McLeod
Project Editor: Virginia McLeod
Editorial Assistant: Maya Birke von Graevenitz
Picture research: Emmanuelle Peri, Jenny Faithfull
Production controller: Leonie Kellman

Design: Hans Stofregen

Printed in China